STEAMPUNK
FASHIONS COLORING BOOK

MARTY NOBLE

DOVER PUBLICATIONS, INC.
MINEOLA, NEW YORK

Steampunk fashion is a reproduction of the clothing that is or could be found in steampunk literature. It is about creating an outfit that delights the senses, entertains the wearer, and engages the viewer. In this intricately detailed coloring book, artist Marty Noble has created thirty-one beautiful images of young women dressed in steampunk style. As part of the *Creative Haven* series for the serious colorist, this book will appeal to all lovers of steampunk and Victoriana.

Bibliographical Note
Steampunk Fashions Coloring Book is a new work, first published by Dover Publications, Inc., in 2015.

International Standard Book Number
ISBN-13: 978-0-486-79748-9
ISBN-10: 0-486-79748-1

Manufactured in the United States by RR Donnelley
79748105   2015
www.doverpublications.com